Rosalind Tompkins-Whiteside's book, *Rare Anointing*, is a mind-to-heart journey to the throne of God as He speaks directly to each of us. Finally here is an answer to the "mystery" of suffering. The beauty that *Rare Anointing* unveils and the peace it radiates truly gives the reader an understanding as to how essential suffering is to spiritual growth and development. This is definitely a book for any season!

—Linda Nickles-Dukes

Pastor Rosalind Y. Tompkins-Whiteside's book *Rare Anointing* offers each of us the chance to recognize "who" we are and "whose" we are. We are all God's children first and we all have experienced some type of suffering in our lives. This book gives us a "rare" opportunity to delve into our sufferings, while recognizing how blessed we are to have suffered. Otherwise, how else would we know how good God really is? Rosalind takes us through her trials and tribulations, and through it all, she still gives God all the honor, glory, and praise. Why? She has been not only through the fire, but also through heartache, pain, longsuffering, and rejection. *Rare Anointing* is a testimony of how *suffering* and sometimes longsuffering can lead to a life of joy, obedience, patience, glory, healing, grace, life, compassion, hope, and relief from suffering through Christ Jesus. *Rare Anointing* shows through God's words and His example that trouble does not last always and that through our pain and suffering the main question is *What lesson do I need to learn?* *Rare Anointing* takes us through Jesus' longsuffering and shows us how Jesus endured. This book challenges us to find our purpose and destiny so that we can become better testimonies and servants for our Lord. *Rare Anointing* helps us to turn our brokenness into blessings!

—BRENDA "BJ" JARMON, PHD

RARE
ANOINTING

RARE ANOINTING

ROSALIND TOMPKINS-WHITESIDE

A STRANG COMPANY

RARE ANOINTING by Rosalind Y. Tompkins-Whiteside
Published by Creation House
A Strang Company
600 Rinehart Road
Lake Mary, Florida 32746
www.creationhouse.com

This book or parts thereof may not be reproduced in any form, stored in a retrieval system, or transmitted in any form by any means—electronic, mechanical, photocopy, recording, or otherwise—without prior written permission of the publisher, except as provided by United States of America copyright law.

Unless otherwise noted, Scripture quotations are from the King James Version of the Bible.

Scripture quotations marked NIV are from the Holy Bible, New International Version. Copyright © 1973, 1978, 1984, International Bible Society. Used by permission.

Scripture quotations marked NLT are from the Holy Bible, New Living Translation, copyright © 1996. Used by permission of Tyndale House Publishers, Inc., Wheaton, IL 60189. All rights reserved.

Hebrew and Greek definitions are from the *New Strong's Exhaustive Concordance of the Bible*.

Cover design by Terry Clifton

Copyright © 2007 by Rosalind Y. Tompkins-Whiteside
All rights reserved

Library of Congress Control Number: 2007920197
International Standard Book Number: 978-1-59979-172-2

First Edition

07 08 09 10 11 — 9 8 7 6 5 4 3 2 1

Printed in the United States of America

To Pastor Helena Barrington who inspired the title for this book and is such a shining example of a woman of God who possesses a "rare anointing."

To all who are suffering, may you find relief within the pages of this book.

I also dedicate this book to my daughter, Janar, who God used mightily to help bring me out of addiction.

Acknowledgments

First of all I thank God for my Lord and Savior Jesus Christ, who inspired me to write this book through the inspiration of the precious Holy Spirit! I would also like to thank my bishop, Dr. Mark J. Chironna, who is the epitome of someone with a rare anointing; my husband Charles, for his support and understanding; my mother Louise; and my fellow laborers in Christ, Renae, Nettie, and Millie. I love you!

Contents

Foreword xiii
Introduction 1
1 A Man of Sorrows 6
2 I Want to Know Him 11
3 Suffering That Leads to Joy 17
4 Suffering That Leads to Obedience 23
5 Suffering That Leads to Patience 30
6 Suffering That Leads to Glory 35
7 Suffering That Leads to Healing 40
8 Suffering That Leads to Grace 45
9 Suffering That Leads to Life 50
10 Suffering That Leads to Compassion 55
11 Suffering That Leads to Hope 60
12 A Rare Anointing 65
13 Relief From Suffering 80
Appendix 85

Foreword

Rosalind Tompkins-Whiteside is one of those rare individuals with a rare anointing indeed. What you are holding in your hands is not simply a book; it is her life, her journey, and her direct experience with God. While the issue of suffering may not be a popular topic, every believer experiences it at one time or another. Whether or not they want to acknowledge it, admit it, and make the most of it is their choice. Rosalind will teach you how to make the most of the struggles and sufferings you endure, and she will give you access to the secrets behind having a rare anointing.

In the pursuit of God's highest and best for your life, Rosalind will clearly let you know that it is impossible to ignore the role that the sufferings of Christ play in your spiritual formation and in your own spiritual quest. As you read through the chapters, take time to meditate on the poems that this woman of God has written and the prayers she invites you to pray. You will find the pathway to peace and assurance in the midst of your challenges. I was mindful as I read through *Rare Anointing* that the City Foursquare in the Book of Revelation has twelve gates, and each gate is made out of a single pearl. For what reason is a pearl worth so much, and what would be the reason for the Holy Spirit signifying that access to the Holy City is by way of twelve gates made of twelve pearls? The reason is quite simple: Pearls are the only precious gems that come into existence out of suffering! An oyster suffers from an irritation that invades its existence and secretes the fluid around the irritation, which becomes a precious pearl. Access to a rare anointing comes out of a willingness to learn obedience, as did Christ in the pain He suffered.

It was Helen Keller who made the following statement about suffering: "Character cannot be developed in ease and quiet. Only through experience of trial and suffering can the soul be strengthened, vision cleared, ambition inspired, and success achieved."[1] You will discover in this powerful little book that you have gained access by faith in Christ to a grace that is inexhaustible, and regardless of the circumstances you may find yourself in, you can always rejoice in the hope of the glory of God. You can choose to learn obedience in suffering. "We also rejoice in our sufferings, because we know that suffering produces perseverance; perseverance, character; and character, hope. And hope does not disappoint us, because God has poured out his love into our hearts by the Holy Spirit, whom he has given us" (Rom. 5:3–5, NIV).

The woman of God who wrote this treatise will carefully take you by the hand and lead you into a safe and secure awareness of the abiding love of God and to your own gateway and access point to things eternal. The key to unlocking that gateway that gives you access to that rare anointing is what you are holding in your hand right now. Rosalind Tompkins-Whiteside was given permission by the One who has taught her so well to give you the key that He gave her to transform her pain into power. Honor the key you are holding and act on it, and your own rare anointing will become evident to all.

—MARK J. CHIRONNA, PHD
ORLANDO, FLORIDA

Introduction

THIS BOOK WILL GIVE you a look at suffering and how it can produce a rare anointing to heal the brokenhearted and set the captives free.

In my book, *As Long as There Is Breath in Your Body, There Is Hope,* there is a chapter in which I discussed the power of suffering that leads to humility. I stated how I was able to embrace suffering in my life by allowing myself to feel pain without self-medicating. "Embracing the suffering for me was to embrace the One who suffered so much at the hand of humanity."[1]

In the pages that follow I will look at the role suffering played in the life of Jesus Christ and the role that suffering plays in our lives. It is through suffering that we can learn many important lessons. Suffering is designed by the Master not to crush but to create. In modern Christianity there is not much room for pain and suffering. Contrastingly, we promote Jesus much like pharmaceutical companies promote their drugs. Their inherent message is, "Take these pills and all of your pain will go away." Oftentimes the church paints a picture that Jesus is some type of elixir for those who are down and out. "Try Jesus and all of your troubles will be gone," is the message that is often portrayed. However I realize from the Word of God that, truthfully speaking, life after Christ is not all "peaches and cream." Even the abundant life that is promised to believers in Christ has pain and suffering as an intricate part of the growth process. I believe that a person who learns the secrets of purposeful suffering, which I will identify throughout the book, comes through with a rare anointing that brings peace, joy, and healing to the brokenhearted, the poor, the rejected, and the despised.

I started using marijuana when I was twelve years old, and I was addicted to some type of mind-altering substance for twelve years straight. I experienced tremendous pain and suffering as a result of my addiction and the subsequent choices that I made. I literally lost my mind on four different occasions and had to be hospitalized in psychiatric hospitals; I experienced the pain of losing a baby that I carried six months in my womb, because she stopped breathing and died; and I was rejected by a man that I loved and was left to carry another baby all alone

Introduction

and then rear her as a single parent. I have now been drug and alcohol free for over twenty years!

Although the things that I went through were very traumatic, I must say that they have helped me to now be a carrier of a rare anointing. Throughout the process of healing and wholeness, I learned secrets of purposeful suffering that I will share in detail in this book. I believe that a rare anointing is produced in the furnace of affliction. Even if the afflictions are of your own making, you can learn from your experiences and allow them to bring you to a place of brokenness and surrender. I have found that to truly live, you must die to self. I had to learn that the things that I experience are to make me and mold me and shape me into the vessel that I was created to be, and that is a vessel that carries a rare anointing.

My Baby Girl

> When you came into my world, my life was a mess and you know that!
> You showed up on the scene all sparkling and clean.
> You were just what I needed to help me really believe that
> It was time to take stock of my life.
> You see, prior to your arrival, I was living like a wild girl, caught in the cycle of addiction.
> Baby girl, you taught me conviction!
> All of a sudden I had another to think of other than myself.

It was through my love for you that Christ's love
    finally shined through
The muck and mire of my life.
Love for my baby girl!
You changed my world with one smile and a cry,
Even the diapers that I would dry helped me to
    see life through different eyes.
I had purpose and destiny lying in my lap before
    me.
As I dreamed of you and I taking life by storm,
Wrapped in the capable arms of our Father who
    is in heaven.
So, as you live your life and grow, please always
    know that I was your life's first mission.
Mission accomplished, baby girl!
Thank you for changing my world!

Rare Anointing

It's oh so special, oh so sweet;
Crowned with glory from head to feet;
Some may say, "How'd you get that way?"
Well, I've been through the fire and I've been
    through the rain;
I've been so confused until I didn't even know
    my own name.
I been up to heaven and, yes, I've been down
    to hell;
I've seen and heard things that I dare not tell.
I wondered, waited, and anticipated;
Looking intently to be emancipated from the
    trials and tribulations that I cocreated, only

Introduction

to find a new state of mind when I realized that it was all for a purpose.

You see, to produce the wine, the grapes must be crushed.

And to produce the oil the olives must be pressed.

And to produce the anointing I must confess;

Something had to die!

Death is painful at its best;

But through the pain I learned to rest and

Trust the Lord through each and every test;

Out of the suffering, out of the pain, I heard the Lord Jesus calling my name. He said, "Rosalind, come forth; I'm here for you. There is something for you to do. The blind must see, the dumb must talk, the deaf must hear, and the lame must walk."

I learned a valuable lesson that I want to share with you.

No matter what you may be going through, no matter how painful, haunting, daunting, or taunting it may be,

Just remember it is producing a *rare anointing* to set the captives free!

Chapter 1

A Man of Sorrows

For he shall grow up before him as a tender plant, and as a root out of a dry ground: he hath no form nor comeliness; and when we shall see him, there is no beauty that we should desire him. *He is despised and rejected of men; a man of sorrows, and acquainted with grief:* and we hid as it were our faces from him; he was despised, and we esteemed him not.
—Isaiah 53:2–3, emphasis added

THIS PROPHECY FROM ISAIAH about Jesus points to the ultimate reason why Jesus came, and that was to sacrifice His life for our sins. As a result of His well-defined purpose and destiny, He suffered along the way until the ultimate suffering during His death on the cross. The word

A Man of Sorrows

sorrows in the scripture above is the Hebrew word *mak'ob,* which means pain and sorrow, both physical and mental. Even though Jesus suffered both physical and mental pain, He was able to complete His mission.

Anybody who has ever been rejected can understand the serious mental and emotional anguish that rejection produces. Rejection is at the root of many serious mental disorders, because belonging and acceptance are inherent human needs. Oftentimes when those needs are not met, there is a void that develops and is replaced with rejection or the fear of rejection ruling and reigning and thus hindering progress. Rejection, if permitted, can immobilize and completely stop you in your tracks.

Jesus "came unto his own, and his own received him not" (John 1:11). Ouch! That had to hurt badly! He could have decided at that point to turn around and abort the mission. How often do you get to a place where you are not accepted and decide to give up? Many of us allow the pain of rejection to determine our actions, but thank God Jesus did not. He understood that the pain and suffering was just a part of the whole. It did not define or determine His outcome. As a matter of fact, I believe that it helped Him to always turn to the Father, who accepted Him, loved Him, and affirmed Him.

In the aforementioned scripture Jesus was described as a man that "hath no form nor comeliness; and when we shall see him, there is no beauty that we should desire him," thus allowing us to see a side of Jesus that many would deem unbecoming to a king. This description of our Savior is definitely not what many in the modern twenty-first-century culture would look for in a leader. To the contrary, most would look for someone who is handsome and desirable, well-liked, and respected. But that is not the package that our Messiah chose to come in. If we are not careful, we could misunderstand the verse to say that Jesus was ugly, depressed, and melancholy all the time. Through Scripture we see that is not the case. As a matter of fact, in the Gospels we see Jesus as a vibrant, compassionate, charismatic leader, despite the things that He suffered.

John gave us a glimpse of Jesus' triumphant entry into Jerusalem:

> On the next day much people that were come to the feast, when they heard that Jesus was coming to Jerusalem, Took branches of palm trees, and went forth to meet him, and cried, Hosanna: Blessed is the King of Israel that cometh in the name of the Lord.
> —JOHN 12:12–13

I have found in my own life experiences that when I turn to the Father, He always affirms me and loves me unconditionally—no matter what anybody else says or does. When I cry out to God, He hears my cry and fills me with love, joy, and peace.

Many of you can relate to the hurt that comes with rejection. A man that I loved rejected me. It hurt so much, I thought I would literally die. Although for me dying wasn't an option, because I was pregnant. I had to find a way to keep on going not just for me, but also for my unborn child. It was during this "night season" in my life that I learned how to cry out to God. Although a man rejected me, the Lord accepted me and loved me unconditionally. It was through that deep experience with Him that I learned to trust Him with my whole heart. As I cried myself to sleep many nights, I realized that I was not alone; therefore, I didn't have to be lonely. Years later, God blessed me with my husband Charles who loves me very much.

Secrets of purposeful suffering

- Allow suffering to cause you to seek the face of God.
- Know that when you cry out to God in your suffering, you are not alone. He is right there with you.

Prayer of Comfort

Father God, we pray right now for You to manifest Your presence and for Your Holy Spirit to rest upon us as we experience rejection issues. We pray that we will turn to You and know that as we seek You, we will find You, because You are always with us. You understand the pain of rejection. As You triumphed over all pain and suffering, so can we as we call on Your name in the time of trouble. Lord, we pray that the pain would not abort the various missions that You have us on and that it will only cause us to lean and depend more on You for Your guidance, acceptance, and protection. In Jesus' name, Amen!

In the Midst of It All

As you live your life going through trials and tests;
There are some things that can cause you great stress;
They come to make you want to give up;
They zap your energy and empty your cup;
But in the midst of it all you can stand tall!
In the midst of it all on Him you must call;
He will hear and answer your cry;
Why don't you just try?
Even if you have had a fall;
He is right there with you in the midst of it all;
Waiting on your call;
Call on Jesus, don't be like King Saul who went to the witch and dug a great ditch into which he did fall!
Seek the Lord; give Him a call because He is right there with you in the midst of it all!

Chapter 2

I Want to Know Him

Suffering is the key that unlocks the door to a secret place of the Most High God. It is in this place or state of being that we truly surrender to His will and not ours. It is also in this place that God is able to strengthen us for the journey. Therefore this place can be identified as a place of surrender and strength. Jesus went to this place on the night before His crucifixion.

The Bible identifies the physical location as the Garden of Gethsemane:

> Then Jesus went with his disciples to a place called Gethsemane, and he said to them, "Sit here while I go over there and pray." He took Peter and the two sons of Zebedee along with him, and he began to be sorrowful and troubled. Then he said to them, "My soul is

> overwhelmed with sorrow to the point of death. Stay here and keep watch with me."
> —Matthew 26:36–39, niv

In the midst of His suffering, Jesus ultimately submitted to the will of the Father over His own will. He said, "Father, if you are willing, take this cup from me; yet not my will, but yours be done" (Luke 22:42, niv). It was also in this place that "An angel from heaven appeared to him and strengthened him" (v. 43). It was necessary for Jesus to stop by the Garden of Gethsemane on His way to the cross, just as it is important for us to go to the place of surrender and strength during times of suffering. I believe that Jesus was able to surrender His will, because He knew the Father intimately and could trust Him completely. The only way that we can get to that place of surrender and strength during times of suffering is by getting to know the Lord.

The apostle Paul said:

> I want to know Christ and the power of his resurrection and the fellowship of sharing in his sufferings, becoming like him in his death, and so, somehow, to attain to the resurrection from the dead.
> —Philippians 3:10–11, niv

The Greek word for fellowship in the above scripture is *koinonia*, which means "fellowship, association, community, communion, joint participation, intercourse." It also means "the share which one has in anything and intimacy." Not only did Paul want to know Christ in the power of His resurrection, but he also wanted joint participation, communion, intercourse, and intimacy while sharing in Christ's suffering. That is powerful! So often we want to know Christ in His power, but how often do we truly want to know Him by sharing in His suffering?

The way we get to the place of surrender and strength during times of suffering is by getting to know Christ in the fellowship of His suffering. We get to know Him by studying the Word of God and finding out what He has to say to us about our situations. We get to know Him by spending time with Him in prayer and ultimately identifying with Him. Identifying with Christ means to associate with Him in feelings and interests. That is to place ourselves in His shoes and feel what He feels. It is through identifying with the Savior that we see that He identifies with our struggles and we realize that we are in this together. As He suffered, we suffered; as we suffer now, so He suffers with us and through us.

> Therefore, since we have a great high priest who has gone through the heavens, Jesus the Son of God, let us hold firmly to the faith we profess. For we do not have a high priest who is unable to sympathize with our weaknesses, but we have one who has been tempted in

> every way, just as we are—yet was without sin. Let us then approach the throne of grace with confidence, so that we may receive mercy and find grace to help us in our time of need.
> —Hebrews 4:14–16, niv

As we get to know Jesus the Christ we see that He does care. By identifying with the Lord's suffering we realize that He understands and He is willing to help us through the pain and suffering in our lives.

When you are going through difficult times, it is common to believe that nobody understands or cares about what you are going through. As you get to know Jesus, you will realize that He does care, and because He cares, you can come to Him and cast your cares upon Him (see 1 Pet. 5:7).

In Matthew 11:27–30 (niv) Jesus said:

> All things have been committed to me by my Father. No one knows the Son except the Father, and no one knows the Father except the Son and those to whom the Son chooses to reveal him. Come to me, all you who are weary and burdened, and I will give you rest. Take my yoke upon you and learn from me, for I am gentle and humble in heart, and you will find rest for your souls. For my yoke is easy and my burden is light.

During tough times we generally tend to be more open to learning about God. I know that for me,

I was wide open after the many things that I suffered. I realized that I needed help, and it was during those seasons in my life that I took the time to really get to know the Lord in a very intimate way. I wouldn't trade those times for anything in the world!

Secrets of purposeful suffering

- Surrender your will to the will of the Father, and allow Him to strengthen you.
- Identify with Christ in your suffering to the point of true intimacy and oneness.

Prayer of Comfort

Father God, we pray right now for You to reveal Your Son to all who are experiencing times of loss, grief, and uncertainty. Lord, we surrender our will to You and pray that You will strengthen us in every area. You know the fragilities of man, and yet You still love us. Lord God, allow us to know beyond a shadow of a doubt that You can identify with everything that we go through. Reveal Yourself, Lord. In Jesus' name, Amen!

I Am the Joy

When I look into the mirror, tell me what do I see?
The reflection of the glory staring back at me!
The essence of Christ is who I see;
And I realize that it is no longer me but we.
For I am the joy that was set before my Lord;
As He hung, bled, and died on the cross for my sins;
Creation cried and thought it was the end.
But today, I know that it didn't end, but begin.
For I am the joy!
As I go throughout my day burdened by the weight of the world;
I stop and realize, as I look into His eyes, that I am the joy!
I am the one that He saw and decided to stay on that cross so that I wouldn't
be lost.
I am the joy, and because I am, I can laugh and not cry; smile and not frown; live and not die!
I can continue to try and try to reach the goal of my soul being with my Savior.
Every day it carries me along the way; just to know that I am the joy!

Chapter 3

Suffering That Leads to Joy

Suffer means "to endure death, pain, or distress."[1] It is important to distinguish between physical pain and emotional pain or distress. Some physical pain can be alleviated with pharmaceutical drugs that block our ability to feel the pain. They can be narcotics or over-the-counter pain relievers. For the examples used in this particular chapter, I am primarily referring to emotional pain and distress. However all suffering is relative. What causes one person pain may not have the same effect on someone else. Nevertheless, we have all felt the hurt of emotional pain. Sometimes it is our fault, and other times it is not. Whether or not it is our fault, the feelings are the same. They are similar no matter what race, gender, age, or socioeconomic status. Pain is universal. The causes may differ, but the feelings are the same.

Our responses to pain may differ as well. In my book, *As Long as There Is Breath in Your Body, There Is Hope*, I talk about those with "bottomless pits" and those with "spiritual leprosy." In both cases the terms identify those with high tolerance for pain. The responses to the pain that they experience do not appropriately alleviate the pain or allow them to learn from the pain. In the bottomless pit example, the pain gets increasingly worse time after time with no end in sight. In the spiritual leprosy example, the pain is numbed out so that it is not felt and therefore isn't dealt with. Neither are good responses to emotional or physical pain. If someone has such a high tolerance for pain that they refuse to get help, they can ultimately die from the pain; whether because of an accident associated with recklessness, or from physical or mental sickness and disease. The body can literally shut down and stop functioning properly when there is too much emotional or physical pain.

Another response to pain and suffering is anger. We can become angry with people, God, the world, and sometimes ourselves. Out of anger we ask "Why me?" or "Why is this happening to me?" While the answers to those questions may or may not be relevant, they are very seldom helpful. Oftentimes they lead to more unanswered questions. The more appropriate question is: "What do I need to learn from this place?" Subconsciously we allow our anger to replace the true feelings of hurt, sorrow, and disappointment, because we can deal with anger outwardly, but pain has to be dealt with inwardly. In other words, we can project our anger toward others, but pain is personal. Revenge, screaming, or fighting brings no relief from pain. When you lash out in anger but are really experiencing pain, there is no relief. If you are not careful, you can become an angry person even if you are a Christian.

In the Garden of Gethsemane, right before going to the cross, Jesus said to the Father, "My Father, if it is possible, may this cup be taken from me" (Matt. 26:39, NIV). *Cup* is the Greek word *poterion* and it means "a cup, a drinking vessel." Or metaphorically, "one's lot or experience, whether joyous or adverse, divine appointments, whether favorable or unfavorable, are likened to a cup, which God presents one to drink: so of prosperity and adversity." Just like Jesus, we often respond to pain by asking for it to be taken away. We say things like, *Lord, please get me out of this!* We need to be like Jesus who also said "Yet not as I will, but as you will" (Matt. 26:39, NIV). In order to say that, there has to be a point of realization that God is the ultimate authority and He has all power. Therefore, He can very well stop the pain at any given moment. He can let the cup of sorrow and pain pass. Oftentimes He doesn't, and I believe the reason that He does not is because He knows that the same cup of pain and sorrow is also the cup filled with pleasure and prosperity. He is the one who made the cup and filled the cup. He knows exactly what we need in order to fulfill the very reason that we have been put on planet Earth. The pain is often not good to you, but it is definitely good for you. It reminds me of the castor oil that my mother used to give me for all kinds of ailments. It tasted nasty, but it worked wonders!

We find in the Bible that the cup that Jesus was referring to was the crucifixion that He was about to endure. He was about to give up everything, including His life, for us. However that is precisely why He came to Earth, therefore, no matter how painful the cup, He knew that ultimately it would be fulfilling and joyous.

We have record of this fact penned by the apostle Paul in the Hebrews 12:2: "Looking unto Jesus the author and finisher of our faith; who for the joy that was set before him endured the cross, despising the shame, and is set down at the right hand of the throne of God." He endured the cross or drank from the cup, because He saw joy set before Him. *Joy* in the referenced verse is the Greek word *chara* and it means "joy, gladness." His joy was His purpose and destiny, the reason why He came—you and me! We were the joy set before Him! We can endure the pain and sufferings that we go through by seeing purpose and destiny before us. We can't do that unless we have our eyes fixed on Jesus, the author and finisher of our faith.

Suffering That Leads to Joy

What you look at is important while you go through pain of any kind. Do not look at the pain itself or the person who you believe caused you the pain. Do not look at the circumstances surrounding the pain. These are the wrong places to look. Look up and live! Look to the hills from which comes your help. Look to the Word of God for comfort. Look to the Holy Spirit who is the Comforter! Look to yourself, deep down on the inside where Christ lives, and draw strength from the inside out. That is where your joy resides. There you will find God-given goals to focus on. That is your destiny. You will be surprised at the power that you have within yourself to heal yourself. Your joy is your purpose and destiny. In 1 Thessalonians 1:6, the apostle Paul wrote, "You became imitators of us and of the Lord; in spite of severe suffering, you welcomed the message with the joy given by the Holy Spirit" (NIV). Even in the midst of the suffering, you can receive joy from the Holy Spirit, and joy brings true relief!

I had a mental breakdown twenty-four years ago because of my addiction to drugs. I had just been released from a mental hospital and was living in Pensacola, Florida, with my mother and father. Occasionally, I would walk to a park and sit by the water on the Pensacola Bay. As I looked out over the bay, I contemplated my future about five years out. I couldn't see anything but darkness ahead. I certainly didn't want to look at my present condition, because it was so gloomy. I was severely depressed. Some days

I would just stay in bed all day and watch television. It wasn't until I began to see myself going back to college in Tallahassee and finishing my degree that I began to have hope for the future.

During times of pain, you must focus on desired outcomes or goals for the future that will give you the power to go through it. You may not be able to see the whole picture, but just get a glimpse of your joy. Your joy could be that career that you were put here to do, that ministry that you were called to, or that family that you were placed into. Your joy is the place in the kingdom of God that only you can fulfill.

Secret to purposeful suffering

▸ Endure the pain by receiving joy from the Holy Ghost while looking unto Jesus for your joy (purpose and destiny).

Prayer of Comfort

Father God, we thank You for Your goodness and mercy. Lord, we are in need of Your miraculous power to come upon us and help us to endure. Lord, You are no respecter of persons. What You have done for me, You will do for all of Your children who believe. Lord, help us to walk by faith and not by sight. Help us to keep our eyes on You and our hearts turned toward heaven. Reveal Your purpose, Your glory, and Your joy to all who are downcast. In Jesus' name, Amen!

Chapter 4

Suffering That Leads to Obedience

I BELIEVE THAT NOTHING HAPPENS by accident. The pain and suffering that we are allowed to go through are for specific reasons. Even the suffering that Jesus went through was definitely not in vain. He learned obedience through the things He suffered.

> During the days of Jesus' life on earth, he offered up prayers and petitions with loud cries and tears to the one who could save him from death, and he was heard because of his reverent submission. *Although he was a son, he learned obedience from what he suffered* and, once made perfect, he became the source of eternal salvation for all who obey him.
> —Hebrews 5:7–9, NIV, EMPHASIS ADDED

Now if Jesus, both the son of man and the Son of God, learned obedience through the things He suffered, so can we. I believe that one of the primary reasons that we suffer as believers in Christ is to learn obedience. I can attest to this fact from some of the personal experiences that I have gone through.

One such experience is the period in my life when, because of my drug use, I miscarried a baby girl. I carried her in my womb for six months, then she just stopped breathing. Even though I was an addict, I still loved my baby. I also loved the Lord, even though I wasn't living for Him at the time. I had to deliver my baby stillborn. That was one of the most devastating experiences that I have ever gone through! The pain was so great because a part of me died.

Although I was in denial of my addiction, deep down I knew that she died because of my drug use. The guilt alone was excruciatingly painful. In the midst of the sorrow, I can honestly say that I learned obedience through what I suffered. I finally realized that my life wasn't a joke and that I needed to stop using drugs and take responsibility. The loss of my baby girl was the beginning of the end of my drug addiction.

However it did take a few more life experiences before I finally stopped using altogether, two years later while I was pregnant with my daughter, Janar. I remembered the pain and suffering that I went through before, and I was able to totally stop using drugs and alcohol for the first time in twelve years! I learned obedience through the things that I suffered.

This process is not just going to happen through osmosis. There has to be a conscious decision made not to allow the suffering to make you hard, but pliable. Obedience is essentially submission to authority. The authority to which we must learn to submit to is the ultimate authority—God. Isn't it interesting that Jesus, though He stated on many occasions that He was here to do the will of the Father and that He only did what He saw the Father doing, still had to learn obedience? In His humanity He had to learn obedience, and so do we. It is human nature to rebel and want to do things our way. You have probably heard the phrase, "It's my way or the highway." Suffering teaches us that it is "God's way or the hard way!" There is a level of submission and surrender that can only be acquired through suffering. Suffering is designed to produce humility.

> Let this mind be in you, which was also in Christ Jesus: Who, being in the form of God, thought it not robbery to be equal with God: But made himself of no reputation, and took upon him the form of a servant, and was made in the likeness of men: And being found in fashion as a man, he humbled himself, and became obedient unto death, even the death of the cross. Wherefore God also hath highly exalted him, and given him a name which is above every name: That at the name of Jesus

every knee should bow, of things in heaven, and things in earth, and things under the earth; And that every tongue should confess that Jesus Christ is Lord, to the glory of God the Father.

—Philippians 2:5–11

Jesus humbled Himself and became obedient. There must be humility before obedience. If not, we can find ourselves just going through the motions with no true change. In James 4:10 the Bible declares, "Humble yourselves in the sight of the Lord, and he shall lift you up." After the humility and obedience comes the exaltation where the Lord raises you up above the suffering and pain! That is exciting!

Humble in these particular verses of Scripture is the Greek word *tapeinoo* and it means "to make low." When suffering leads to obedience the result is a humble and contrite spirit. The Bible states in Isaiah 57:15, "For thus saith the high and lofty One that inhabiteth eternity, whose name is Holy; I dwell in the high and holy place, with him also that is of a contrite and humble spirit, to revive the spirit of the humble, and to revive the heart of the contrite ones." *Contrite* in this particular scripture is the Hebrew word *daka'*, which means "to crush." It is from this state of being that God Himself dwells with us to revive us. *Revive* in this particular scripture is the Hebrew word *chayah* and it means "to live, have life, remain alive."

Suffering That Leads to Obedience 27

Suffering comes in degrees. It can be suffering because your flesh is being denied or suffering because you are in the pigpen like the prodigal son depicted in the Bible. Either can produce obedience in a true believer in Christ. In the parable of the lost son we see how suffering helped the young man to come to his senses.

> And he said, A certain man had two sons: And the younger of them said to his father, Father, give me the portion of goods that falleth to me. And he divided unto them his living. And not many days after the younger son gathered all together, and took his journey into a far country, and there wasted his substance with riotous living. And when he had spent all, there arose a mighty famine in that land; and *he began to be in want*. And he went and joined himself to a citizen of that country; and he sent him into his fields to feed swine. And he would fain have filled his belly with the husks that the swine did eat: and no man gave unto him. And when he came to himself, he said, How many hired servants of my father's have bread enough and to spare, and I perish with hunger! I will arise and go to my father, and will say unto him, Father, I have sinned against heaven, and before thee.
> —Luke 15:11–18, emphasis added

The word *want* in the above scripture is the Greek word *hustereo*, and it essentially means "to be left behind in the race and so fail to reach the goal." Metaphorically, it means to fail to become a partaker. It also means to suffer want, to be devoid of, to lack (be inferior) in excellence and worth. The young man in this parable was suffering on two main levels.

First of all, he suffered from a fall from grace. By taking his inheritance early and leaving his father's house, he went from being a son to acting like a beggar. Secondly, because of the famine and the fact that he had spent all his money with riotous living, he was literally hungry and in need of food. It was through this intense experience that he learned many life lessons, which led him back to his father's house. The Bible doesn't specifically say, but I imagine that although the father obviously loved him dearly, there were rules that he had to live by. I believe that is the essence of why he left home. He wanted to live life on his terms, not his father's. Jesus gave this parable to depict the love that God the Father has for all of His children. It is also indicative of how we as believers sometimes leave the Father's house so we can go and live as we please, out from under the commandments and principles of the Bible. But just like the young man in the parable, we see that it is hard living apart from the covering of the Father, and thus we too can learn obedience through the things we suffer.

Secret to purposeful suffering

▸ Humble yourself and learn obedience to Christ Jesus and His Word through the things that you suffer.

Prayer of Comfort

Father God, You love us so much, and we are eternally grateful that Your love never fails. Help us to accept Your love and learn from the mistakes, trials, and tribulations that we go through. Teach us obedience. Help us to humble ourselves under Your mighty hand that You might exalt us in due time. And help us to realize that it is better to obey than to sacrifice. Lead us and guide us into all truth, and forgive us for the times that we have rebelled against You and Your Word. In Jesus' name, Amen!

CHAPTER 5

SUFFERING THAT LEADS TO PATIENCE

IN MANY CHRISTIAN CIRCLES we often hear the phrase, "The patience of Job." The reason is because he was a man depicted in the Bible that endured much hardship, pain, and sorrow. The New Testament makes reference to how the prophets of old who spoke in the name of the Lord are examples to us of "patience in the face of suffering" (James 5:10–11, NIV). Job's testimony epitomizes the power of endurance and perseverance under extreme circumstances. Although Job lost everything including his health, the Bible says that he did not curse God and die. He continued to wait on the Lord, and he said in Job 14:14 "All the days of my hard service I will wait for my renewal to come" (NIV). Job did wait, his change came, and he received double for his trouble.

You can learn patience in the midst of suffering when you learn how to wait on the Lord. You must believe and have hope that God is good and that He is going to change you and the situations that you are facing. Oftentimes we want God to change the circumstances when we should be asking for Him to change us. God wants Christ to be formed in you, and that is a painful process that takes time and patience.

One might ask the question, "Oh Lord, how long do I have to take this?" or simply, "How long, Lord?" These are very common questions that are often asked in the midst of suffering. When we ask these questions, we imply that it is the Lord who is determining the time limit of our suffering. While God is sovereign, I have learned that it is not always a matter of God's timing, but ours. In other words, the better questions to ask are, "What now, Oh Lord?" "What would You have me do?" and, "What would You have me to learn while experiencing trials and tribulations?" As the Lord reveals His will to us, we learn how to wait on Him as one waits on tables in a restaurant. By that I mean we learn how to get busy serving the Lord and His purpose for our pain. As we do this we learn patience.

I quit my job to start the ministry, Mothers in Crisis, Inc. I knew that was what the Lord wanted me to do; however, I was not prepared for the suffering that I had to endure as a result. I thought that when I quit my job, the Lord would have other resources available for me to pay my bills while starting the ministry. Well, for a long time that was simply not the case. I went through a period when I only had ice in my refrigerator to feed my daughter and myself. As I look back on that experience, I realize that the Lord had to teach me to lean and depend on Him for everything. I learned how to hear the voice of the Lord like never before through fasting and prayer. During that period in my life, I learned how to trust God and truly wait on Him. It wasn't an easy season, but God was faithful. At the appointed time, He blessed me with a position at Florida A & M University, where I could work and still start Mothers in Crisis.

God does not get pleasure from our suffering. It is not His will for us to be hurt, mistreated, and abused. That is not the kind of God we serve. I do not believe that it is the Lord's will for anyone to stay in an abusive relationship. That is why it is very important to ask the Lord, "What would You have for me to do?" What I am referring to is suffering for purpose and destiny. In the Bible we find this type of suffering identified in many scriptures, one of which is found in James 1:2–4: "Consider it pure joy, my brothers, whenever you face trials of many kinds, because you know that the testing of your faith develops perseverance [patience]. Perseverance must finish its work so that you may be mature and complete, not lacking anything" (NIV). This scripture is not talking about going through trials and tribulations just for the sake of suffering. No, there is something that we can gain, a treasure that we could not receive otherwise.

Secret to purposeful suffering

▸ Believe that what you suffer is for a purpose, and therefore you can have patience and wait on the Lord!

Prayer of Comfort

Lord God, we thank You that You are longsuffering with us, and You are a very patient Father. Help us to be patient with You and trust You through the things that we suffer, knowing that they are producing the character in us that is like You. Help us to learn patience through the things that we go through. Help us, dear Lord, to be those that will wait on You and be of good courage. In Jesus' name, Amen!

Genocide

Children dying
Mothers crying
Women raped
No escape
Where to hid?
It's genocide!

Jesus died
Shed His blood
Rose again
So we can win
Against all sin!

Help is coming
Letter writing
Outraged sighing
What to do?
It's up to you!

Praying and fasting
Listening and speaking
We won't stop until someone's keeping
Watch over the children of the world.

God bless the children!

Chapter 6

Suffering That Leads to Glory

We all have experienced pain and persecution for different reasons—race, gender, socioeconomic status, or some type of handicap. No matter what the cause, it hurts to be rejected, talked about, or ostracized for any reason.

As a child, I was taunted and teased, because I walk differently than most people. My knees turn in instead of being straight. Growing up, I remember being talked about because of the way I walked. At home, at school, and in the neighborhood I was called names. For a long time I was very self-conscious about walking before people. I believe that self-consciousness helped contribute to my smoking marijuana at the age of twelve years old.

When I was high, I was not self-conscious, and I didn't care what people said or thought about the way I walked. Everything was funny to me when I was stoned. It wasn't until I accepted Christ that I was truly able to accept myself with all my flaws and imperfections. Through Christ I learned how to love myself just the way I am, because that is how God made me, and He doesn't make junk! In Christ's love and acceptance I realized that I didn't need drugs to feel good about myself. If you are experiencing persecution because of some real or perceived imperfection, please know that Christ loves you just the way you are, and allow His love to comfort, heal, and cover you.

The Bible talks about suffering for a much higher call. That is suffering because of who you are in Christ Jesus. Suffering that leads to glory is suffering for Christ's sake, not your own. The early church, as depicted in the Bible, experienced extreme persecution. Many people lost their lives because of their belief and devotion to Christ. Many Christians living in the United States of America do not understand the magnitude of persecution and suffering that Christians endure today in various countries throughout the world. There are multitudes of Christians who live in fear for their very lives, but they serve and trust the Lord anyway. You may wonder how they can do it. I believe that it is because of the glory that rests upon believers who suffer for Christ's sake.

Suffering That leads to Glory

Dear friends, do not be surprised at the painful trial you are suffering, as though something strange were happening to you. But rejoice that you participate in the sufferings of Christ, so that you may be overjoyed when his *glory* is revealed. If you are insulted because of the name of Christ, you are blessed, for the *Spirit of glory and of God rests on you.* If you suffer, it should not be as a murderer or thief or any kind of criminal, or even as a meddler. However, if you suffer as a Christian, do not be ashamed, but praise God that you bear that name. For it is time for judgment to begin with the family of God; and if it begins with us, what will the outcome be for those who do not obey the gospel of God? And, "If it is hard for the righteous to be saved, what will become of the ungodly and the sinner?" So then, those who suffer according to God's will should commit themselves to their faithful Creator and continue to do good.

—1 Peter 4:12–19, NIV

For our light affliction, which is but for a moment, worketh for us a far more exceeding and eternal weight of glory; While we look not at the things which are seen, but at the things which are not seen: for the things which are seen are temporal; but the things which are not seen are eternal.

—2 Corinthians 4:17–18

The Greek word for *glory* as we see it in the scriptures referenced is *doxa* and it means "opinion, judgment, view." It also means splendor. Therefore those who partake in the sufferings of Christ can expect to partake in His glory, splendor, grace, and majesty during the suffering and after the suffering when His glory is revealed in us. That is exciting! The glory of the Lord is the tangible presence of God manifested to His people. Just to know that God's manifested presence is available to you as you suffer with Him for righteousness sake is enough to bring comfort and strength.

Secret to purposeful suffering

- Realize His tangible presence (glory) is with you during times of suffering to destroy the yokes of bondage, depression, oppression, and hopelessness.

Prayer of Comfort

Lord, we thank You that we are not alone when we face trials, tribulations, and sufferings because of Christ. We thank You for Your glory that is resting upon us right now. We thank You that the glory of the Lord will be revealed in us to protect us from all hurt, harm, and danger. Lord, please allow your glory to cover all who are suffering for Christ's sake. In Jesus' name, Amen!

I Believe in Miracles

In this day and age of skepticism,
Racism, materialism, sexism, and atheism;
I believe in miracles!
In this day and age of haters, players,
Cocaine, hurricanes, gas prices off the chain;
I still believe in miracles!
You see it started with a miracle when Jesus was conceived,
And the miracles continued the moment I believed,
That there was a way out of darkness and the hell that I was in.
The moment I was born again and made Jesus my friend,
The light was turned on so no matter what is going on;
I believe in miracles!

Chapter 7

Suffering That Leads to Healing

For this is thankworthy, if a man for conscience toward God endure grief, suffering wrongfully. For what glory is it, if, when ye be buffeted for your faults, ye shall take it patiently? but if, when ye do well, and suffer for it, ye take it patiently, this is acceptable with God. For even hereunto were ye called: because Christ also suffered for us, leaving us an example, that ye should follow his steps: Who did no sin, neither was guile found in his mouth: Who, when he was reviled, reviled not again; when he suffered, he threatened not; but committed himself to him that judgeth righteously: Who his own self bare our sins in own body on the tree, that we, being dead to sins, should live unto righteousness: by whose stripes [a bruise, wale, wound that trickles with blood] ye were healed.

—1 Peter 2:19–24

Suffering That Leads to Healing

> But he was wounded for our transgressions, he was bruised for our iniquities: the chastisement of our peace was upon him; and with his stripes we are healed.
>
> —Isaiah 53:5

Jesus' suffering on the cross bought us healing in our bodies. Because He took on our sins and paid the price of them through the crucifixion, we can now be healed! That is good news! Healing is made available through Jesus' suffering. He already suffered for whatever sickness and disease there has been or will ever be. We can take the finished work on the cross and apply it to our lives and receive our healing. You may say, "How can I do that?" That is a very good question, and the answer is by faith. You have to believe that Jesus Christ's healing anointing did not stop when He went back to heaven. No, it continues throughout eternity because of the finished work on Calvary. Through the Holy Spirit of promise, God's healing presence is here today.

I have experienced God's healing power in my life on numerous occasions. One of which is the time the Lord healed my mind. He actually gave me a new mind. It was during the period of my life when I was addicted to drugs and experiencing hallucinations. As a result I had to literally be hospitalized in psychiatric wards on four different occasions. I'll never forget the time that I was in Jackson Memorial in Miami. I had just experienced the worst episode ever, and I had to be taken to the hospital by the police in a strait jacket. It wasn't until my family came and prayed for me in a circle of prayer that I began to come back to myself. Overnight I was able to think clearly, and I became aware of my surroundings. I can honestly say that from that time until now—and that was over twenty years ago—I have been healed!

One way to apply Jesus' healing to our lives is through communion. In 1 Corinthians 10:16, the Bible states, "The cup of blessing which we bless, is it not the communion of the blood of Christ? The bread which we break, is it not the communion of the body of Christ?" And Jesus Himself states in John 6:56–57, "He that eateth my flesh, and drinketh my blood, dwelleth in me, and I in him. As the living Father hath sent me, and I live by the Father: so he that eateth me, even he shall live by me."

When we partake in communion we are symbolically eating His flesh and drinking His blood. *Communion* in the above referenced scripture is the Greek word *koinonia* (which also translates as *fellowship* as stated earlier in the book), and it essentially means "the share which one has in anything, participation, intercourse, fellowship, intimacy." We have a share in Christ's redemptive work on the cross. He didn't stay in the grave. He rose again on the third day. Therefore we don't have to stay in the valley; we can rise again through His resurrection power into newness of life! Jesus is the Lily of the Valleys (see Song of Sol. 2:1). So while you are in the valley, just look at your beautiful Savior and remember that weeping might endure for a night, but joy is coming in the morning (see Psalm 30:5). The healing power of the Lord Jesus Christ is coming!

Secret to purposeful suffering

▸ Apply the blood of Jesus to your life and receive God's healing power.

Prayer of Comfort

Lord, we thank You for Your finished work on Calvary. As a result, we know that by Your stripes, we are healed. Lord, we apply that healing to our lives and the lives of those who are suffering from sickness and disease in their bodies. Lord, we receive Your miraculous healing power by faith right now. We declare that the blood of Jesus is applied, and healing is released. Lord God, please relieve and remove all pain and anguish of body, soul, and mind. In Jesus' name, Amen!

Temptation

And I said, "Lord, deliver me.
I wish I could be like that tree,
Standing tall with no feelings at all!"
But You gently said to me, "If you were indeed like that tree,
Then there'd be no need for Me!
Take it easy, fast and pray, remember Me in all you do and say.
It takes faith and patience to run this race, and don't forget my grace is sufficient.
For when you are weak, I am strong. I'm here to help when things go wrong!
Take the time to renew your mind.
Submit your will and your body too,
Then you will receive power to make it through,
Any and all temptations that come to you!
Submit to Me, resist the devil and he will flee!"
And I said, "Lord, thank You much,
I now receive Your touch, Your love, Your strength, and Your grace!
I now have power to run this race.
For when I am weak, You are strong,
Your power helps me to carry on!"

Chapter 8

Suffering That Leads to Grace

GRACE IS THE UNMERITED favor of God. It is also the power of God to save and keep those who believe in the Lord Jesus Christ. Oftentimes when we experience trials and tribulations in our lives, there is a tremendous amount of guilt, shame, and judgment associated with why we are going through what we are going through. People that are close to us often judge us and determine that it is somehow our fault that we are suffering.

In the Book of Job we see Job's friends judging him and blaming him for his condition. Sometimes we blame ourselves, even if we have no control over the situations that we are facing. In the case of sickness and disease, we sometimes feel as though we would be healed if we just had more faith. Blame, guilt, and shame are all negative emotions that tend to exasperate, rather than help, the problem. Negative emotions release negative energy that stops the flow of God to heal and strengthen. That is why grace is so important!

> And lest I should be exalted above measure through the abundance of the revelations, there was given to me a thorn in the flesh, the messenger of Satan to buffet me, lest I should be exalted above measure. For this thing I besought the Lord thrice, that it might depart from me. And he said unto me, *My grace is sufficient for thee: for my strength is made perfect in weakness.* Most gladly therefore will I rather glory in my infirmities, that the power of Christ may rest upon me. Therefore I take pleasure in infirmities, in reproaches, in necessities, in persecutions, in distresses for Christ's sake: for when I am weak, then am I strong.
> —2 CORINTHIANS 12:7–10, EMPHASIS ADDED

God's grace is the power of God to strengthen when we are experiencing painful situations. God's love does not blame and beat you down for being weak; it builds you up and allows you to rest in His strength that is made perfect in weakness. That is powerful!

Because of God's grace we do not have to be afraid to go to the Lord. He cares and understands and is just waiting on us to approach Him with boldness.

Suffering That Leads to Grace

> Seeing then that we have a great high priest, that is passed into the heavens, Jesus the Son of God, let us hold fast our profession. For we have not an high priest which cannot be touched with the feeling of our infirmities; but was in all points tempted like as we are, yet without sin. *Let us therefore come boldly unto the throne of grace, that we may obtain mercy, and find grace to help in time of need.*
> —Hebrews 4:14–16, emphasis added

God's grace is available to help you through all pain and suffering. It is through your trials that you can truly understand the meaning of grace. The times that you are not at your best, God still loves you and is desirous of your company. When we are weak, then He is strong; when we fall, He picks us up, because His grace is waiting to be released in our lives. The only thing you have to do is ask and you will receive the power needed to go through any trial or tribulation in grace, with grace, by grace, and through grace!

Secret to purposeful suffering

▸ Allow His grace to be sufficient to carry you through any trial and tribulation.

Prayer of Comfort

Lord, we thank You for Your grace. May it be released right now without measure into the hearts and minds of Your people to strengthen and help during these trying times. Father God, we bind every spirit of negativity, blame, condemnation, and guilt in Jesus' name, and we release the grace needed to run this race. Amen!

Transformation

The caterpillar wonders why he can't fly;
Crawling around with his head hanging down, wearing a frown;
Inside he sees wings like none he's ever seen;
Flying high through the sky among the trees;
But in reality day after day he crawls around dodging birds of prey;
But inside he sees wings like none he's ever seen;
Flying high through the sky among the trees;
One day he believes as he sees the wings that they belong to him;
He pictures himself flying and a process begins trying to make him become what he was born to be;
The process of transformation is finally taking him off the ground and into the trees;
Flying high through the sky with wings like none he's ever seen,
But now he possesses and his soul caresses life as it is supposed to be;
No more crawling around with his head hanging down, wearing a frown;
He now has his wings to fly high through the sky way up in the trees;

Suffering That leads to Grace

You may be like that caterpillar living your life crawling around with your head hanging down, wearing a frown.

Jesus came to give you your wings so you too can fly high, through the sky, way up in the trees.

Look inside where Christ resides and see the new creation that you were born again to be.

Allow the process of transformation to begin taking you off the ground and into the trees,

Flying high in the Spirit with wings like none you've ever seen.

But now you possess and your soul can caress life and that more abundantly!

Chapter 9

Suffering That Leads to Life

For if you live according to the sinful nature, you will die; but if by the Spirit you put to death the misdeeds of the body, you will live, because those who are led by the Spirit of God are sons of God. For you did not receive a spirit that makes you slave again to fear, but you received the Spirit of sonship. And by him we cry, "Abba, Father." The Spirit himself testifies with our spirit that we are God's children. Now if we are children, then we are heirs—heirs of God and co-heirs with Christ, if indeed we share in his sufferings, in order that we may also share in his glory. I consider that our present sufferings are not worth comparing with the glory that will be revealed in us.

—Romans 8:13–18, NIV

Suffering That Leads to Life

The suffering that the Bible refers to is suffering in the flesh. The Greek word for flesh in the referenced scripture is *sarx*, and it means, "the flesh, denotes mere human nature, the earthly nature of man apart from divine influence, and therefore prone to sin and opposed to God." Whenever we deny ourselves, there is suffering. There has to be death to the earthly, natural desires that are apart from God's will for our lives in order to not live according to the flesh. How many of you know that it hurts to die? Any time we say no to the flesh and yes to the Spirit we suffer in the body just as Christ suffered in His body for our sins. But it is precisely through this suffering that we live. We can live in the Spirit when we die to the flesh.

I am reminded of the time in my life when I stopped using drugs and alcohol completely after using daily for about twelve years. Boy did my flesh hurt! I had headaches every day, and I was very irritable. Some days I would have given just about anything to smoke a marijuana joint, but I thank God I didn't. It was during that period of my life, over twenty years ago, that I totally surrendered my will to the Lord. I was pregnant with my daughter, Janar, who is now nineteen. I learned a lot during that experience. Mainly I learned the fact that I wouldn't die if I didn't get high. I learned to say no to my flesh, no matter how it hurt. Now if I could just learn to say no to chocolate, I would be all right!

It is very important to learn how to deny the flesh, no matter how you feel. It is through saying no to fleshly desires that we truly say yes to life. Sex before marriage, gluttony, addictions, and excessiveness are just a few fleshly endeavors that we must learn to reject. Through fasting and prayer we can train ourselves to deny the flesh. When we truly realize that what we lose is nothing compared to what we gain through this process of suffering, it becomes easier. We gain freedom as opposed to bondage, health as opposed to sickness and disease, and life as opposed to death when we deny our flesh.

This way of thinking is diametrically opposed to the world's way of thinking or behaving. Some of the messages that are portrayed on television and other media are, "If it feels good, do it"; "I did it my way"; "Play now, pay later"; and "Just do it." All of these, along with the images that we see in music videos and movies, seem to imply that to deny your every want or desire is crazy. Sin, not denial, is in! But we know the truth as revealed in the Word of God.

> Therefore, since Christ suffered in his body, arm yourselves also with the same attitude, because he who has suffered in his body is done with sin. As a result, he does not live the rest of his earthly life for evil human desires, but rather for the will of God.
> —1 Peter 4:1–2, niv

Through Christ we are changed into a new creature that no longer lives according to the dictates of the world, flesh, or devil.

Secret to purposeful suffering

▸ Deny your flesh so that your spirit can live!

Prayer of Comfort

Lord God, please help us to deny our fleshly desires, even though it hurts to do so. Help us to be those that are willing to suffer in our bodies in order to live the life that Jesus died to give us. Help us to realize that if we die to our flesh, we can be resurrected by the Spirit of God into newness of life in Christ. In Jesus' name, Amen!

Shining Star

There are those in this world who desire fortune and fame. They want everyone to know and say their names. I want to be a star in the mantra of the day. Obsession with their work and their play is what we see each and every day. Day after day, we are bombarded through the media: television, radio, video, DVDs, Internet, CDs, newspapers, iPods, and magazines, the same old names and faces show up on the scene.

I have lived long enough to know and realize as I look into the eyes of our future that it's not about money fortune or fame. And who gives a flip who knows your name, if you don't' take time to help someone along the way? To me that is the order of the day!

The true stars are those who give money and time. When you help others then you really shine, bright as the morning on a hot summer's day. Keep on shining as you help others along the way. Your reward is coming and is already here as lives are blessed because you care!

Chapter 10

Suffering That Leads to Compassion

Times of crisis can help to bring people and nations together because of the common thread of suffering. We saw that on September 11, 2001, when the terrorist attack on America resulted in over three thousand deaths as the Twin Towers in New York City crumbled before our very eyes. The images of the airplanes crashing into the buildings are seared in America's consciousness forever. The severe devastation and loss brought about an outpouring of love, heroism, prayer, and support that was undeniable. Even people who were primarily concerned only with themselves began to think about others and God. Everywhere you traveled in America you could see signs saying, "God Bless America," and, "Pray for America." In August 2005, when Hurricane Katrina ripped through New Orleans, Louisiana and parts of Mississippi were totally wiped out, America cried while seeing the images of bodies floating lifelessly on the floodwaters as people on rooftops waited for help. Once again there was a tremendous outpouring of compassionate help, even in the midst of rioting, finger-pointing, and utter horror at the extent of the damage and loss.

As we learn to lean and depend on the Lord Jesus Christ through our suffering we become qualified to help and bring comfort to others as they suffer.

> Praise be to the God and Father of our Lord Jesus Christ, the Father of compassion and the God of all comfort, who comforts us in all our troubles, so that we can comfort those in any trouble with the comfort we ourselves have received from God. For just as the sufferings of Christ flow over into our lives, so also through Christ our comfort overflows. If we are distressed, it is for your comfort and salvation; if we are comforted, it is for your comfort, which produces in you patient endurance in the same sufferings we suffer. And our hope for you is firm, because we know that just as you share in our sufferings, so also you share in our comfort.
> —2 Corinthians 1:3–7, niv

We realize from the Word of God that our sufferings are shared sufferings and our comfort is

Suffering That leads to Compassion

shared comfort. Who better to share your sufferings with than those who are going through what you are going through or what you have gone through? That is the power of the support group movement—the realization that others who have similar trials and tribulations can gain strength and support by sharing the load.

When I started Mothers in Crisis over fifteen years ago, it started out as simply a support group for women in recovery. I had been clean for four years at that time, and I knew I needed to be with others who could relate to where I had been. I also had a strong desire to help those who were yet suffering with the disease of addiction. Over the years I have seen time and time again the power of suffering when it leads to compassion for others. It may not be the exact same issues, but as long as you can relate on the level of pain that it produces, you can bring hope. Relating on the level of pain is getting in touch with your feelings and becoming compassionate to the feelings of others. On many occasions the Bible states that when Jesus healed the sick, He was moved with compassion.

> And there came a leper to him, beseeching him, and kneeling down to him, and saying unto him, If thou wilt, thou canst make me clean. And Jesus, *moved with compassion,* put forth his hand, and touched him, and saith unto him, I will; be thou clean. And as soon

as he had spoken, immediately the leprosy departed from him, and he was cleansed.
—MARK 1:40–42, EMPHASIS ADDED

Compassion in the referenced scripture is the Greek word *splagchnizomai*, and it means, "to be moved as to one's bowels, hence to be moved with compassion, have compassion (for the bowels were thought to be the seat of love and pity)." When Jesus helped others, it wasn't from His head, but from His heart.

There is something about suffering that makes one able to empathize, not just sympathize, with others. Being able to put yourself in another's position and thus feel what another feels is a gift of suffering. When we experience suffering on an individual level, it is imperative to realize that the suffering is not just an isolated incident. Inevitably the suffering that we face is the same suffering that many others face daily. When I was addicted to drugs and alcohol, I lost a baby because of my drug usage. I carried her for six months. When she stopped breathing, I had to deliver her stillborn. I was crushed by this incident, and I finally began to realize that my addiction wasn't a joke. I remember writing in my journal, "Why, God? I know this pain that I am experiencing is not all in vain." It wasn't until years later that I understood that what I went through was not only for me, but also for the thousands of others that I would be able to minister hope to.

Secret to purposeful suffering

- Share in others' sufferings and comfort with compassion.

Prayer of Comfort

Lord God, please help us to realize that there are others who are going through the same things that we are. They need us to share with them in their sufferings and bring comfort to them through hope in the Lord Jesus Christ. Lord, please forgive us for any selfishness, and help us to know that our suffering is not in vain. In Jesus' name, Amen!

Chapter 11

Suffering That Leads to Hope

Therefore being justified by faith, we have peace with God through our Lord Jesus Christ: By whom also we have access by faith into this grace wherein we stand, and rejoice in hope of the glory of God. And not only so, *but we glory in tribulations also: knowing that tribulation worketh patience; And patience, experience; and experience, hope: And hope maketh not ashamed*; because the love of God is shed abroad in our hearts by the Holy Ghost which is given unto us.
—Romans 5:1–5, emphasis added

THE EXPERIENCE THAT WE gain through trials, tribulations, and suffering can give us hope. When we reflect back on the goodness of the

Lord and how He brought us out and sustained us through one thing, then we know He can and will bring us out of anything that we may face! Therefore we don't have to be ashamed. Think about the goodness of the Lord during your present suffering, and you will have hope.

There was a time in my life when it seemed like I got myself into something that I could not shake, no matter how hard I prayed and tried. It wasn't until I started meditating on what God had already done for me in the past that I began to have hope for my situation. I began to think about how He delivered me from drugs, gave me my mind back after I lost it time and time again, and blessed me with my baby girl, Janar. The list goes on and on of His goodness to me! After thinking about all the experiences where God came through for me, I had hope and said, like the prophet Jeremiah, "Is anything too hard for [God]?" (Jer. 32:27, NIV). No matter what you are going through, it is not too much for you and God to handle!

Hope is needed in order to sustain sanity in the face of suffering and pain. People often give up because they lose hope. The Bible states in Proverbs 13:12, "Hope deferred makes the heart sick, but a longing fulfilled is a tree of life" (NIV). When all hope is gone, the problems get worse, because of our mental state of being. We often say things like, "What's the use?" or, "I might as well give up." Both of these statements are signs of hopelessness and a "sick heart."

At the heart of all pessimistic thinking is hopelessness. Pessimism often leads to sarcasm. At the heart of sarcasm is pain, because pain that is left to fester causes one to lash out at others.

I am known for saying, "As long as there is breath in your body, there is hope." People who are suffering often say, "Where is hope? I am going through hell and I don't see, have, or feel hope!"

Where Is Hope?

> Hope is found in the breath that I breathe;
> In the stars in the sky and in the cool of the breeze.
> Hope is found in a baby's cry; or tears rolling down the eye,
> Of one who knows that every good thing flows from the heart of God.
> Hope is found in the birds that sing, in the grass as it grows,
> In the smell of a rose, in the dew as it settles upon the ground.
> Hope can be found in the middle of pain, in the streets of frustration,
> And in the home of the name that is above every name!
> Hope is found when you hear the name, think the name, or say the name,
> It's all the same!
> Because, Jesus IS HOPE!

Suffering That leads to Hope

I wrote this poem after listening to a discussion on a national public radio show. The guests were outlining current events and sharing their insights on issues relating to race and violence. As I sat listening, I asked myself, *As an African-American leader in my community, what would I say about the state of affairs in urban communities throughout the United States if I were a part of that discussion?* As I got out of my car, I looked up and began to speak this poem in response. No matter how bad it looks, there is still hope, and we can find it not in anger, blaming, or rhetoric, but in life, living, and Jesus.

The meaning of the first part of the poem is that hope is found all around. Hope can be found in the common, simple things in life that are often overlooked and taken for granted. For example, when you breathe, there is the implied hope that you will breathe again. When you look up in the sky and see stars, there is the implication that light shines even in darkness. When you hear a baby cry there is the knowledge of life. When tears roll down your eye, it represents the fact that you can feel and are yet alive. When your hear birds, see grass, smell roses, and feel dew, they are signs of nature saying there is a reason to sing, that things are growing, and cleansing comes from above. The second part of the poem implies that even in difficult times of pain and frustration, hope can still be found, and it identifies hope personified in the Person of Jesus Christ!

But I would not have you to be ignorant, brethren, concerning them which are asleep, that ye sorrow not, even as others which have no hope. For if we believe that Jesus died and rose again, even so them also which sleep in Jesus will God bring with him. For this we say unto you by the word of the Lord, that we which are alive and remain unto the coming of the Lord shall not prevent them which are asleep. For the Lord himself shall descend from heaven with a shout, with the voice of the archangel, and with the trump of God: and the dead in Christ shall rise first: Then we which are alive and remain shall be caught up together with them in the clouds, to meet the Lord in the air: and so shall we ever be with the Lord. Wherefore comfort one another with these words.

—1 Thessalonians 4:13–18

Secret to purposeful suffering

▸ Allow the suffering to lead you to hope in Jesus.

Prayer of Comfort

Father God, please help us have hope in the midst of all the pain. Help us to not give up, but continue to allow you to manifest hope in our hearts and mind. Help us to always remember your goodness and mercy and keep our eyes fixed on you through it all. In Jesus' name, Amen!

Chapter 12

A Rare Anointing

RARE MEANS VERY UNCOMMON, remarkable, and excellent. To *anoint* means to rub or smear on oil for consecration. In Isaiah 10:27 the Bible states, "And it shall come to pass in that day, that his burden shall be taken away from off thy shoulder, and his yoke from off thy neck, and the yoke shall be destroyed because of the anointing" (NIV).

Anointing in this particular verse of scripture is the Hebrew word *shemen* and it means "fat, oil, olive oil, as staple, medicament or unguent, for anointing, and metaphorically; (of fruitful land, valleys)."

In 2 Corinthians 1:21–22 the Word of God declares, "Now it is God who makes both us and you stand firm in Christ. He anointed us, set his seal of ownership on us, and put his Spirit in our hearts as a deposit, guaranteeing what is to come" (NIV). Jesus declared in Luke 4:18–19, "The Spirit of the Lord is on me, because he has anointed me to preach the good news to the poor. He has sent me to proclaim freedom for the prisoners and recovering of sight to the blind, to release the oppressed, to proclaim the year of the Lord's favor" (NIV).

Anointed in these two verses of scripture is the Greek word *chrio*, and it means "to anoint, consecrating Jesus to the Messianic office, and furnishing him with the necessary powers for its administration, and enduing Christians with the gifts of the Holy Spirit." The anointing has purpose. God anoints us by smearing us with the Holy Spirit to destroy the yokes of bondage and set the captives free. The Holy Spirit's power is the source of the anointing manifested in our lives.

We find in the Bible that olive oil was one of the ingredients used in the anointing process. It was used for consecrating a priest, king, or tabernacle in the Old Testament and it was used for anointing a sick person to be healed in the New Testament. Even today in many churches olive oil is still used as an intricate part of prayer.

One of the interesting things about olive oil is the process by which the oil is produced. The olives are pressed and crushed beyond recognition in order to secrete the oil. The process is quite detailed and debilitating to the olive. That is precisely what happens to us as we allow ourselves to go through the process of pain and suffering that leads to the release of a rare anointing to set the captives free.

There is a crushing of will and spirit that allows the essence of humility and worship to be released. It is in this place that the Holy Spirit dwells. The reason that I say it is rare is because you simply do not find it that often. It is hard to find someone who has been crushed beyond recognition, so humbled until one can say just like the apostle Paul said, "I no longer live, but Christ lives in me" (Galatians 2:20, NIV). I believe that the apostle Paul could say that because of the things that he suffered.

> For we would not, brethren, have you ignorant of our trouble which came to us in Asia, that we were pressed out of measure, above strength, insomuch that we despaired even of life: But we had the sentence of death in ourselves, that we should not trust in ourselves, but in God which raiseth the dead: Who delivered us from so great a death, and doth deliver: in whom we trust that he will yet deliver us.
> —2 CORINTHIANS 1:8–10

Because of the tremendous suffering and persecutions that he faced, I believe the apostle Paul was definitely one who possessed a rare anointing.

There are five characteristics of a person with a rare anointing that I would like to explore in detail at this time: **P**ower, **E**ndurance, **D**epth, **L**ove, and **R**elationship. PEDLR is an acronym that I have coined to identify the rare anointing that I am referring to. A peddler is a person who distributes goods and services in a very transient way. A kingdom PEDLR (pronounced peddler) is one who distributes the anointing of the King to various people as he or she travels along the way. PEDLRs are produced in the furnace of affliction; however, when they come forth the anointing that they possess is as pure gold. We definitely need more PEDLRs in the kingdom of God.

Power is a characteristic of a person with a rare anointing. Power comes from God to save, heal, and deliver. One of the Greek words for *power* in the New Testament is *dunamis* and it means "strength, power, ability, inherent power, power residing in a thing by virtue of its nature, or which a person or thing exerts and puts forth." It also means "power for performing miracles." We find this particular Greek word for power used in Acts 1:8-9, "But ye shall receive power, after that the Holy Ghost is come upon you: and ye shall be witnesses unto me both in Jerusalem, and in all Judaea, and in Samaria, and unto the uttermost part of the earth."

We can see from the scripture that this power is released after the Holy Spirit comes upon you. This is the power of the Holy Ghost, not human power or ability to make things happen. We can also ascertain that this power makes you bold, because the Bible says after receiving the power from the Holy Ghost you will become witnesses of God. A witness is a person who has firsthand knowledge about a thing that they have seen or experienced for themselves.

As you experience God through the Person of the Holy Spirit, it gives you something to talk about. You can't help but talk about the goodness of the Lord, and as you share, His power is released to save, heal, and deliver! Now that is powerful! A person with a rare anointing understands the power of their testimony. They realize the need to share with others what they have gone through, because others are going through the same things, and they need to know that there is hope. Therefore a person with a rare anointing becomes bold for Christ. They don't let pride keep them from being real and authentic about the things they have suffered. Salvation, healing, and deliverance are all miracles that are manifested through their lives, first in them, and then increasingly in others whose lives they touch. Power to walk right, talk right, and live right is released through God into their lives.

Endurance is also a characteristic of a person with a rare anointing, primarily because they have learned how to endure in the midst of extreme pressure. Sometimes while experiencing trials and tribulations, a thought may come to mind that says, *You might as well end it all*. Unfortunately, too many people give in to thoughts such as these and commit suicide. The suicide rate is increasing among teenagers and young adults, even those who are Christians. I believe that it is because people have a tendency to give up hope and believe the lie that whatever they are facing is simply too much to bear.

When I was pregnant with my daughter, Janar, I felt so alone. As stated earlier in the book, I was also kicking a major drug habit. The moment I found out I was pregnant, I stopped using drugs and alcohol completely. For the first time in twelve years, I was drug free. I was also very depressed. I worked in the Tallahassee Mall administering surveys to consumers about various products. I worked all day and went home at night to a lonely apartment. On many occasions, I would cry myself to sleep at night. I also thought about committing suicide, but the life that was growing inside of me kept me alive. I knew that I had to live for my baby. No matter how bad things may seem, there is always something or someone to live for!

The problem is that we don't always see it. That is where endurance comes in. Second Timothy 2:3 says, "Endure suffering along with me, as a good soldier of Christ Jesus" (NLT). The Greek word for *endure* in this passage of scripture is *kakopatheo*, and it means, "to suffer (endure) evils (hardships, troubles) and to be afflicted." When we learn how to endure, we can stand the tests and trials that we suffer.

The Bible also says, "But those who endure to the end will be saved" (Matt. 24:13, NLT) *Endure* in this passage of Scripture is the Greek word *hupomeno*, and it means, "to remain, to tarry behind, abide."

A Rare Anointing

A rare anointing is produced in a person who learns how to endure. It is rare, because so many people give up right before their breakthrough. They leave God and the place or situation that He has ordained for them to experience. They say, "This is too much," or, "It's too hard." I always say, "This is a lot, but not too much for me and Jesus to handle!"

Depth is a characteristic of a person with a rare anointing. People who have gone through pain and suffering tend to be deeper in terms of their life and living because of what they have experienced. Surface Christianity is no longer an option, because they understand the urgency of making the most of every moment. They are not carried along with the hype of ministry and people, because they have a rare ability to cut to the core. As a result, they receive great revelation of scriptures and things pertaining to the Spirit.

The Bible says in Psalm 42:7, "Deep calls unto deep." The Spirit of God will lead us to the deep things or spiritual things of God as it states in 1 Corinthians 2:9–10:

> But as it is written, Eye hath not seen, nor ear heard, neither have entered into the heart of man, the things which God hath prepared for them that love him. But God hath revealed them unto us by his Spirit: for the Spirit searcheth all things, yea, the deep things of God.

The deep things of God are the things that a person with a rare anointing will continue to pursue in order to receive all that God has for them. Shallowness of thinking and living are seen as fruitless deeds of darkness. When Jesus walked this earth, we see from Scripture that even at the age of twelve years old He was about His Father's business (see Luke 2:49). To be about your heavenly Father's business is to imply a depth of character that puts God where He should be, and that is first, number one, and before all! It is about pursuing God and not allowing anyone to stand in your way of fulfilling your purpose and destiny. A person with depth of spirit is not satisfied with just learning a few clever cliques; they have a realness about them that intimidates some who are not willing to get past the cliques and hype of Christianity.

Although depth is a characteristic of a person with a rare anointing, it does not mean that they are "too heavenly minded to do any earthly good." To the contrary, a person with depth is very useful in the kingdom, because the spiritual revelation and guidance that they receive from the Spirit of God produce results with the least amount of effort on their part. Therefore, they actually do more, because they are Spirit-led and are oriented by grace, not works.

Love is manifested in a person with a rare anointing, because that is the motivating force behind all they do. Love for God and love for their neighbors are the two commandments that they operate from.

They often ask the question, "Where is the love?" A person with a rare anointing understands the power of unconditional love. The God kind of love that compelled Him to send His only begotten Son in order to save humanity is unconditional love. As it states in John 15:12–13, "This is my commandment, That ye love one another, as I have loved you. Greater love hath no man than this, that a man lay down his life for his friends." This kind of love is not selfish. You cannot carry a rare anointing and be selfish, because it is not about you. It's about God and what He desires. Selfishness hinders the anointing. Love compels you to get out of self and into the will of God for your life and others. There is no greater force in this world than love, because God is love.

> Beloved, let us love one another: for love is of God; and every one that loveth is born of God, and knoweth God. He that loveth not knoweth not God; for God is love.
> —1 JOHN 4:7–8

Another component to love is the love that leads to holiness. In John 14:15 Jesus said, "If ye love me, keep my commandments." This implies a love relationship that is so great until it affects your behavior. God wants us to serve Him and do His will because we love Him, not because we have to. Love should be the motivating force of holiness, not rules, doctrines, and regulations. That is why Romans 8:2

states, "For the law of the Spirit of life in Christ Jesus hath made me free from the law of sin and death." We couldn't keep the law as it was under the Old Covenant; therefore, Jesus came and summed everything up into two commandments, both of which are to love, first God and then our neighbors as we love ourselves (see Matt. 22:37–40).

Hebrews 12:14 states, "Follow peace with all men, and holiness, without which no man shall see the Lord." The Greek word for *holiness* in this scripture is *hagiasmos*, and it means "consecration, purification, the effect of consecration and sanctification of heart and life." Holiness is to be set apart unto God and away from the world. This type of living can only be successful if it is motivated by love for God, His Word, and His will. When you are a person that is motivated by love and not law, you are operating in the love that caused God the Father to send His Son into this world. It was because of love.

When we choose the right over the wrong because of love, we release a power that cannot be penetrated. We release the power of love to save, heal, and deliver others as well as ourselves. A person who suffers for love's sake, by experiencing the pain of dying to fleshly desires that war against the spirit, walks in this realm of love and can be used greatly by God! Once love is truly in operation, it produces a rare anointing that cannot be denied.

I first experienced this type of love when I fell in love with Jesus. Have you ever heard the phrases that "love will make you do right" and "love will make you do wrong?" And "if loving you is wrong, I don't want to be right?" I find that those statements ring true. It is because of my love for Him that I want to please Him in every way. Therefore, when things are manifested in me that aren't pleasing to God, I don't stop until they are dealt with through prayer and repentance. This is a continuous process that is motivated by love, not law.

Relationship with the Father, Son, and Holy Spirit is essential in possessing a rare anointing. Knowing who you are as a child of God will cause you to walk as a son or daughter of God. You will have the confidence and authority that comes with being a son or daughter and not merely a servant. Times of suffering and pain can result in knowing the Lord intimately. And it is in that intimacy with Him that we can begin to understand who we are in Christ Jesus. We can see our position in the kingdom of God and the body of Christ.

Having healthy relationships with others in the body of Christ is also a key component in possessing a rare anointing. No man is an island. We need each other! The centurion in the New Testament identified himself as a man under authority (see Matt. 8:9); therefore, he possessed authority and had command over others.

To walk in true authority you must be submitted under authority. There are too many people in the body of Christ who desire to be on top but are not willing to submit to the authority that God places in their lives to cover them and help them grow. They end up in rebellion without even realizing it. The anointing flows downward from God and those that He places in our lives to cover us. A picture of this is found in Psalm 133:

> Behold, how good and how pleasant it is for brethren to dwell together in unity! It is like the precious ointment upon the head, that ran down upon the beard, even Aaron's beard: that went down to the skirts of his garments; As the dew of Hermon, and as the dew that descended upon the mountains of Zion: for there the LORD commanded the blessing, even life for evermore.

Unity is essential for the anointing to pour. I have lived long enough to experience the loss of relationships. I have also lived long enough to realize the importance of true relationships that are based upon mutual love and respect. Oftentimes the very relationships that have the power to produce great fruit for the kingdom of God are the ones that the enemy destroys. Our enemy (identified as Satan in the Bible) hates agreement, because he understands the power of agreement. The Bible states in Matthew 18:19, "Again I say unto you, That if two of you shall agree on earth as touching any thing that they shall ask, it shall be done for them of my Father which is in heaven."

That is powerful! All it takes is agreement to move the heart of God. The Bible also states in Amos 3:3, "Can two walk together, except they be agreed?" We can't even walk with others when there is disagreement. We also can't walk with God unless we agree even when we don't understand. We must agree that He is the sovereign Lord and ultimate authority in our lives. We must also agree that "All scripture is given by inspiration of God" (2 Timothy 3:16).

Relationship with God produces a rare anointing that cannot be shaken. There are many gifted and talented individuals in the body of Christ; however, oftentimes that's all they have. If you take the gifts and talents away, there is nothing left. Relationship with God is the vehicle through which the anointing should flow, not out of a particular gifting.

> Not every one that saith unto me, Lord, Lord, shall enter into the kingdom of heaven; but he that doeth the will of my Father which is in heaven. Many will say to me in that day, Lord, Lord, have we not prophesied in thy name? and in thy name have cast out devils? and in thy name done many wonderful works? And then will I profess unto them, I never knew you: depart from me, ye that work iniquity.
> —MATTHEW 7:21–23

Knowing Him is the most important thing, because it is through our relationship with Him that we can know and do His will. There are times in all of our lives when we can feel alone and that nobody cares, especially during times of suffering. It is in those times that we can establish a strong bond with the Lord and realize that He does care and that He is right there. Once you "taste and see that the LORD is good" (Ps. 34:8), you can develop a hunger and thirst for more of Him.

As you receive more and more of the Lord, you become filled with His glory, and that is the precise ingredient that you need to walk in a rare anointing. A person who knows their God intimately is a person that can be used mightily by Him with substance and force that comes from relationship with Him. Everything that Jesus did as He walked the earth was attributed to His Father. In John 14:10 Jesus states, "Believest thou not that I am in the Father, and the Father in me? the words that I speak unto you I speak not of myself: but the Father that dwelleth in me, he doeth the works." A person with a rare anointing truly understands the concept that it is God who does the work and not them. They give Him the glory that is due His name. They are not trying to make a name for themselves. They are lifting up the name that is above every name, and that name is Jesus!

Prayer of Comfort

Lord God, please help us to be carriers and PEDLRs of Your rare anointing. Help us to realize that You do the work in and through us. Help us to be those who possess power, endurance, depth, love, and relationship with You. In Jesus' name, Amen!

Chapter 13

Relief from Suffering

Prayer brings comfort and gives hope to those who are experiencing trials and tribulations of any kind. The Bible states that we are to "pray without ceasing" (1 Thess. 5:17). This is particularly important during times of pain and suffering, because that is how we are able to walk through the "valley of the shadow of death" without fear (Ps. 23:4).

It is through prayer that we find true relief. Prayer opens the door for God's power to be released in our lives. Please pray these prayers with me for everyone who is suffering. I believe as the Bible declares that the "effectual fervent prayer of a righteous man availeth much" (James 5:16).

The following prayers are inspired by the Holy Spirit and are designed to carry you into the secret place of the Most High God in order to find peace, healing, joy, grace, and help in the time of need.

> *Father God, we pray right now for You to manifest Your presence and for Your Holy Spirit to rest upon us as we experience rejection issues. We pray that we will turn to You and know that as we seek You, we will find You and see that You are right there with us, because you understand the pain of rejection. As You triumphed over all pain and suffering, so can we as we call on Your name in the time of trouble. Lord, we pray that the pain would not abort the various missions that You have us on, and that it will only cause us to lean and depend more on You for Your guidance, acceptance, and protection. In Jesus' name, Amen!*

> *Father God, we pray right now for You to reveal Your Son to all who are experiencing times of loss, grief, and uncertainty. Lord, we surrender our will to You and pray that You will strengthen us in every area. You know the fragilities of man, and yet You still love us. Lord God, allow us to know beyond a shadow of a doubt that You can identify with everything that we go through. Reveal Yourself, Lord. In Jesus' name, Amen!*

> *Father God, we thank You for Your goodness and mercy. Lord, we are in need of Your miraculous power to come upon us and help us to endure. Lord, You are no respecter of persons. What You have done for me, You will do for all of Your children who believe. Lord, help us to walk by faith and not by sight. Help us to keep our eyes on*

You and our hearts turned toward heaven. Reveal Your purpose, Your glory, and Your joy to all who are downcast. In Jesus' name, Amen!

Father God, You love us so much. We are eternally grateful that Your love never fails. Help us to accept Your love and learn from the mistakes, trials, and tribulations that we go through. Teach us obedience. Help us to humble ourselves under Your mighty hand that You might exalt us in due time. And help us to realize that it is better to obey than to sacrifice. Lead us and guide us into all truth, and forgive us for the times that we have rebelled against You and Your Word. In Jesus' name, Amen!

Lord God, we thank You that You are longsuffering with us and You are a very patient Father. Help us to be patient with You and trust You through the things that we suffer, knowing that they are producing the character in us that is like You. Help us to learn patience through the things that we go through. Help us, dear Lord, to be those that will wait on You and be of good courage. In Jesus' name, Amen!

Lord, we thank You that we are not alone when we face trials, tribulations, and sufferings because of Christ. We thank You for Your glory that is resting upon us right now. We thank You that the glory of the Lord will be revealed in us to protect us from all hurt, harm, and danger. Lord, please allow Your glory to cover all who are suffering for Christ's sake. In Jesus' name, Amen!

Prayer of Comfort

Lord, we thank You for Your finished work on Calvary. As a result, we know that by Your stripes we are healed. Lord, we apply that healing to our lives and the lives of those who are suffering from sickness and disease in their bodies. Lord, we receive Your miraculous healing power by faith right now. We declare that the blood of Jesus is applied and healing is released. Lord God, please relieve and remove all pain and anguish of body, soul, and mind. In Jesus' name, Amen!

Lord, we thank You for Your grace. May it be released right now without measure into the hearts and minds of Your people to strengthen and help during these trying times. Father God, we bind every spirit of negativity, blame, condemnation, and guilt in Jesus' name, and we release the grace needed to run this race. Amen!

Lord God, please help us to deny our fleshly desires, even though it hurts to do so. Help us to be those that are willing to suffer in our bodies in order to live the life that Jesus died to give us. Help us to realize that if we die to our flesh, we can be resurrected by the Spirit of God into newness of life in Christ. In Jesus' name, Amen!

Lord God, please help us to realize that there are others who are going through the same things that we are and need us to share with them in their sufferings and bring comfort to them through hope in the Lord Jesus Christ. Lord, please forgive us for any selfishness and help us to know that our suffering is not in vain. In Jesus' name, Amen!

Father God, please help us have hope in the midst of all the pain. Help us to not give up but continue to allow You to manifest hope in our hearts and mind. Help us to always remember Your goodness and mercy and keep our eyes fixed on You through it all. In Jesus' name, Amen!

Lord God, please help us to be carriers and PEDLRs of Your rare anointing. Help us to realize that You do the work in and through us. Help us to be those who possess power, endurance, depth, love, and relationship with You. In Jesus' name, Amen!

Appendix

Secrets of Purposeful Suffering

- Allow suffering to cause you to seek the face of God.
- Know that when you cry out to God in your suffering, you are not alone. He is right there with you.
- Surrender your will to the will of the Father, and allow Him to strengthen you.
- Identify with Christ in your suffering to the point of true intimacy and oneness.
- Endure pain by receiving joy from the Holy Ghost while looking to Jesus for your joy (purpose and destiny).
- Humble yourself and learn obedience to Christ Jesus and His Word through the things that you suffer.
- Believe that what you suffer is for a purpose, and therefore you can have patience and wait on the Lord.

- Realize His tangible presence (glory) is with you during times of suffering to destroy the yokes of bondage, depression, oppression, and hopelessness.
- Apply the blood of Jesus to your life and receive God's healing power.
- Allow His grace to be sufficient to carry you through any trial and tribulation.
- Deny your flesh so that your spirit can live.
- Share in others' sufferings, and comfort with compassion.
- Allow the suffering to lead you to hope in Jesus.

Notes

Forward

1. Helen Keller quote available online at: http://www.quoteworld.org/quotes/7543 (accessed 2/7/07).

Introduction

1. Rosalind Y. Tompkins, *As Long as There Is Breath in Your Body, There Is Hope* (Lake Mary, FL: Creation House, 2005), 64.

Chapter 3

1. *Merriam-Webster's Collegiate Dictionary*, 11th ed., s.v. "Suffer."

About the Author

Pastor Rosalind Y. Tompkins-Whiteside was born and reared in Pensacola, FL, to Louise and Charles Clark. She is the mother of Janar Shenale Tompkins and wife of Pastor Charles Jerome Whiteside. She is a prophetic poet with a compilation of her poems on the *Poems of Life* and *Poems of Life* volume two CDs. She is also the author of *As Long as There Is Breath in Your Body, There Is Hope*.

Pastor Rosalind graduated in 1987 with a bachelor of science degree in social work from Florida State University, and she was first ordained as a minister of the gospel in 1996. Since then, she has worked in the field of prevention, intervention, and treatment for numerous years and is very involved in many community initiatives. Pastor Rosalind is truly a pioneer; in April 1991 she founded Mothers in Crisis (a non-profit community-based grassroots organization comprised of women and men in recovery from drugs and alcohol). She currently serves along with her husband at Turning Point International Church, Inc., (T.P.I.C.). T.P.I.C. is a member of the Legacy Alliance Fellowship of churches and Dr. Mark J. Chironna is the presiding bishop.

Pastor Rosalind loves the Lord with all her heart, mind, and soul. Her hobbies include writing, reading, walking in nature, and communing with God. Pastor Rosalind is an anointed and appointed servant of God who has twelve years of personal experience with drug addiction and has been drug and alcohol free for over twenty years. She stands for hope that is birthed through experience and nourished by love. She stands for hope that shines bright in the midst of darkness, hope that reaches down to the depths of despair and pulls families back from the brink of destruction.

Pastor Rosalind can be seen and heard locally on the Fire & Ice Extreme for Christ and the *Mothers in Crisis in the House* radio and television broadcasts.

Because of Pastor Rosalind's community service and compassionate heart, she was appointed by Governor Jeb Bush to serve on the Commission for Volunteerism for the State of Florida in 2005. She is currently a part of the Tallahassee Chamber of Commerce's Leadership Tallahassee Class 24. In fact, Ms. Tompkins-Whiteside has been the recipient of numerous awards and recognition over the years, including the International Who's Who of Entrepreneurs Award (2000), the Woman of Courage Award from Tallahassee Community College (2001), the Martin Luther King Jr., Humanitarian Award (2002), the Florida A & M University African American Heritage President's Award (2003), NAACP Black Achievers Award in (2003), a resolution recognizing her as an Outstanding Spiritual and Community Leader by the Leon County Board of County Commissioners in (2004), a Delta Sigma Theta Alumnae Chapter Public Service Award in (2005), and a Black Public Administrators Social Service Award in (2006).

Contact Information

Rosalind Y. Tompkins-Whiteside
Mothers in Crisis, Inc.
1500 Lake Avenue
Tallahassee, FL 32310

1-866-430-1050
Ryt2@aol.com
www.mothersincrisis.com